McCOMB PUBLIC LIBRARY
McCOMB, OHIO

D0571674

☙ PROFILES OF GREAT ❧

BLACK AMERICANS

Civil Rights
Leaders

☙❧

Edited by Richard Rennert

Introduction by Coretta Scott King

⦀A Chelsea House
⦀Multibiography

Chelsea House Publishers
New York   Philadelphia

Copyright © 1993 by Chelsea House Publishers, a division of
Main Line Book Co. All rights reserved. Printed and bound in the
United States of America.

First Printing

1 3 5 7 9 8 6 4 2

Library of Congress Cataloging-in-Publication Data

Civil Rights Leaders/Edited by Richard Rennert.
p. cm.—(Profiles of Great Black Americans)
Includes bibliographical references and index.
Summary: Presents brief biographies of eight people involved in
the civil rights movement, including James Weldon Johnson, Martin Luther King, Jr., Thurgood Marshall, and Jesse Jackson.
ISBN   0-7910-2051-7
        0-7910-2052-5 (pbk.)
     1. Civil rights workers—United States—Biography—
Juvenile literature. 2. Afro-Americans—Biography—Juvenile
literature. 3.Afro-AmeriScans—Civil rights—Juvenile literature.
4. Civil rights movements—United States—History—20th century—Juvenile Literature. [1. Civil rights workers. 2. Afro-
Americans—Biography.] I. Rennert, Richard. II. Series.
E185.96.C55 1993   92-37655
323'.092'273—dc20   CIP
[B]   AC

McCOMB PUBLIC LIBRARY
McCOMB, OHIO
NO. J93-5%

❧ CONTENTS ❧

Introduction   4

Jesse Jackson   5

James Weldon Johnson   12

Martin Luther King, Jr.   19

Malcolm X   26

Thurgood Marshall   33

Adam Clayton Powell, Jr.   40

Asa Philip Randolph   47

Walter White   54

Further Reading   61

Index   62

❦ INTRODUCTION ❦

by Coretta Scott King

This book is about black Americans who served society through the excellence of their achievements. It forms a part of the rich history of black men and women in America—a history of stunning accomplishments in every field of human endeavor, from literature and art to science, industry, education, diplomacy, athletics, jurisprudence, even polar exploration.

Not all of the people in this history had the same ideals, but I think you will find something that all of them had in common. Like Martin Luther King, Jr., they all decided to become "drum majors" and serve humanity. In that principle—whether it was expressed in books, inventions, or song—they found something outside themselves to use as a goal and a guide. Something that showed them a way to serve others, instead of only living for themselves.

Reading the stories of these courageous men and women not only helps us discover the principles that we will use to guide our own lives but also teaches us about our black heritage and about America itself. It is crucial for us to know the heroes and heroines of our history and to realize that the price we paid in our struggle for equality in America was dear. But we must also understand that we have gotten as far as we have partly because America's democratic system and ideals made it possible.

We are still struggling with racism and prejudice. But the great men and women in this series are a tribute to the spirit of our democratic ideals and the system in which they have flourished. And that makes their stories special and worth knowing.

JESSE JACKSON

Civil rights leader and poli-
tician Jesse Jackson was born Jesse Louis Burns
on October 8, 1941, in Greenville, South Carolina.
Throughout his youth, he was painfully aware that
white supremacy ruled Greenville. Racial segregation
touched every aspect of life.

Jesse's mother, Helen Burns, was 16 years old and
unwed when he was born; his father, Noah Robinson,

was married to another woman. So Helen raised the baby herself, with the help of her own mother.

Two years later, Jesse's mother married Charles Jackson, a 24-year-old postal worker. Jesse soon learned who his blood father was, but he was to experience many years of rejection before Noah Robinson welcomed him into his home. In the meantime, Charles Jackson was an attentive stepfather, and he legally adopted Jesse and gave him his last name in 1957.

From the time Jesse Jackson was a small child, he was bright, industrious, and a devoted churchgoer. He did especially well in school. At all-black Sterling High School, he was an honor student, a top athlete, and a participant in a variety of extracurricular activities.

After graduating in 1959, Jackson received a football scholarship to the University of Illinois. Disturbed at the lack of racial equality he found in the integrated North, he transferred after his freshman year to North Carolina Agricultural and Technical University, a black state college in Greensboro. He was well aware that eight months prior to his arrival, four of the school's freshmen had sat down at a whites-only lunch counter and had requested service. Their protest had sparked the sit-in movement, which had spread quickly over much of the South.

Jackson was welcomed at his new college, where he became quarterback of the football team, an honor student, and student body president. He soon fell in love with fellow student Jacqueline Davis, and they were married shortly after she discovered she was pregnant. She gave birth to their first child in July 1963; four more children would follow.

By 1963, Jackson had become president of the North Carolina A&T student body. He had also turned into a prominent student activist against racial segregation in downtown Greensboro, leading protest marches sponsored by the Congress of Racial Equality (CORE). He was arrested during one of these demonstrations and spent several weeks in jail. The protests were successful, however: the city desegregated its downtown.

After graduating from college in 1963 with a degree in sociology, Jackson turned down a scholarship to Duke University Law School. Instead, he entered Chicago Theological Seminary on a fellowship. He had decided to follow generations of preachers in the Robinson family and make a career in the ministry.

The call of the civil rights movement proved too strong, though, and in the spring of 1965, six months before his graduation, Jackson's life took a bold turn. He decided to drop out of the seminary and join the nation's most influential civil rights leader, the Reverend Martin Luther King, Jr., and many members of the organization King founded, the Southern Christian Leadership Conference (SCLC), in their drive to register black voters. Although the federal civil rights act signed by President Lyndon B. Johnson in 1964 had ended segregation in restaurants, theaters, and hotels throughout the South, blacks were still prevented from voting in many southern states.

On Sunday, March 7, 1965, King and 600 of his supporters attempted to march from Selma, Alabama, to the state capitol in Montgomery to dramatize their mission. Local and state policemen beat them back using tear gas, clubs, and cattle prods. Jackson saw the proceedings on television, followed by an appeal from King to clergymen across the nation to come join the march. Jackson left Chicago and went straight to Selma.

A natural leader, Jackson stepped immediately into the front ranks of the demonstrators and assumed a take-charge role. After a successful march to Montgomery, which ultimately led to the passage of the Voting Rights Act of 1965, he asked to be appointed to the SCLC staff. King, a bit wary of the headstrong 23-year-old, placed him on the payroll in Chicago under SCLC official James Bevel.

Back in Chicago, Jackson took charge of the local Operation Breadbasket, part of the SCLC's effort to force major companies patronized by blacks to return their patronage in the form of jobs and investments. He promptly recruited more than 200 ministers to carry on this campaign throughout Chicago, with resounding success. King was so impressed that he put Jackson in charge of the entire Operation Breadbasket program.

King then turned his attention to the plight of northern blacks, many of whom lived in dilapidated, inner-city slums. He launched a new campaign of nonviolent demonstrations in Chicago in the summer of 1966, leading marches to City Hall and through all-white neighborhoods to lobby against segregated housing. Jackson emerged as a key player in these protests.

He also proved to be an energetic leader. Jackson's fiery speeches at Operation Breadbasket rallies won him a steady stream of supporters across the country and brought him national fame. Finally, in 1971, he announced that he was resigning from the SCLC to form his own organization, Operation PUSH (People United to Save [later changed to Serve] Humanity).

Borrowing Operation Breadbasket's goal of economic growth for blacks, PUSH organized protest marches, trade fairs, and forums on everything from tax reform to voter registration during the 1970s. It also participated in politics, supporting candidates for local, state, and national offices "committed to human, economic, and social programs." And in 1975, Jackson turned the focus of PUSH from economics to education, launching PUSH-Excel, a campaign designed to encourage young blacks to stay in school, abandon drugs, and develop a sense of self-esteem.

Jackson's organizational skills and mesmerizing speaking style eventually propelled him to the national political stage. In October 1983, having witnessed several months of encouraging support for his candidacy—"Run, Jesse, run," they pleaded—he officially announced that he would seek the Democratic party's nomination for president. He had no trouble attracting media attention. At Christmastime, he achieved a stunning coup when he traveled to the Middle East and negotiated the release of a black U.S. naval aviator who had been shot down and held prisoner by Syria.

Jackson's political fortunes plummeted less than two months later, however, when he appeared at a Nation of Islam rally and said nothing in response to Black

Muslim leader Louis Farrakhan's open threats to
the nation's Jews. Jackson subsequently denounced
Farrakhan's message, but the incident damaged his
campaign, and he captured only 21 percent of the
popular vote and just 11 percent of the delegates in
the Democratic primaries.

Although Jackson did not get his party's nomination
in 1984, he was allowed to address its convention. And
what a speech it was! Broadcast on prime-time television, it electrified blacks and many whites across the
nation as he called for an end to racism and discrimination of every sort—including anti-Semitism—
and urged Americans to take the moral high ground.
"Our time has come!" he urged.

For the 1988 presidential election, Jackson organized his forces into the National Rainbow Coalition
and traveled constantly across the country, building
grass-roots support. By the end of March, he was the
front-running candidate. He won primaries and swept
caucuses.

In the end, Jackson outran and outlasted every
Democratic rival but one: Governor Michael S.
Dukakis of Massachusetts. At their party's conven-
tion, Jackson delivered another spellbinding speech,
just like he had done four years earlier, telling
America, "Keep hope alive."

In 1989, Jackson and his family moved from
Chicago to Washington, D.C. The following year, he
was elected "shadow senator" from the District of
Columbia, a new post created by the city government
to lobby Congress for statehood. He took time out
from that post in August 1990, after Iraqi leader Saddam Hussein invaded Kuwait and imprisoned several

thousand Americans and other foreigners. Jackson flew to Baghdad and successfully negotiated the release of nearly 300 hostages.

And so Jesse Jackson continues to play a major role on the world stage. From meeting with world dignitaries, to getting blacks to vote in record numbers for the 1992 presidential election, to stumping for Democratic candidate Bill Clinton, he remains America's most powerful presence in the fight for racial justice.

JAMES WELDON JOHNSON

$\mathbf{A}$ leading figure in American literature and politics, James Weldon Johnson was born on June 17, 1871, in Jacksonville, Florida. His mother, the former Helen Dillet, was a native of the Bahamas and of mixed black and French descent; his father, James, Sr., was born a free black in Virginia. While James, Jr., was growing up in the booming resort town of Jacksonville, his mother worked as a schoolteacher and his father as the headwaiter at an elegant hotel.

Racial segregation was strictly enforced in Jacksonville. But unlike many southern towns, the city boasted a thriving black community that proved very active in civic affairs. The Johnson children—James Weldon; his younger brother, John Rosamond; and an adopted older girl, Agnes—were taught by their parents to value education. And the local school for blacks that the two boys attended was considered one of the best in the country.

Young Johnson was an avid reader, played the piano and guitar, and frequently joined in neighborhood games of baseball and marbles. Because Jacksonville did not have a high school for blacks, he was sent by his parents to the preparatory division of Atlanta University, in Georgia, to get the equivalent of a high school education after graduating from primary school in 1887. Johnson thrived at his new school and entered the university three years later.

In college, Johnson excelled in his studies, sang in the glee club, wrote poetry, and emerged as an outstanding orator. While teaching in a rural Georgia school during summer vacations in 1891 and 1892, he observed the difference between his cultural and educational background and that of the black sharecroppers' children. Yet he felt a bond with them and began to consider making the fight for racial equality his life's mission.

Johnson graduated from Atlanta University in 1894 at the top of his class and was offered a scholarship to Harvard Medical School. He chose instead to accept the principalship of his primary school back in Jacksonville. A career in education, he believed, would be of greater service to his people.

Johnson succeeded in improving the school during his five years as principal. But he would always be a man of many interests, and so he continued to write poetry, founded a daily newspaper for Jacksonville's black community, and became one of the first blacks to pass the Florida bar exam. He opened a law office with the help of a friend in the summer of 1898 but soon discovered that he lacked a passion for legal work.

To divert himself from his duties as principal and his law practice, Johnson began writing the lyrics for *Tolosa*, a comic opera his brother was composing. Rosamond, who had studied at the New England Conservatory of Music and had become an accomplished pianist and music arranger, worked as a music teacher, choir director, and organist in Jacksonville. In mid-1899, shortly after the opera was completed, the two brothers traveled to New York City to have the songs from *Tolosa* published as sheet music.

While in New York, the Johnsons befriended musician Bob Cole and teamed up with him to write a love song, "Louisiana Lize." A well-known singer bought the rights to the tune, and it became a hit. There would be many others, for the two brothers soon formed a successful songwriting partnership with Cole. By the early 1900s, royalty payments for their work were beginning to roll in, and Cole and the Johnson Brothers was recognized as one of the leading songwriting teams in New York.

All of the Johnsons' tunes were popular, but a song that they cowrote back in Jacksonville proved the most lasting of them all. "Lift Every Voice and Sing," which evokes racial pride and the hope for a better future, was finished in early 1900, while James was still serving as a public school principal. In the years that followed, black organizations across the nation adopted the song and turned it unofficially into the black national anthem. It later became the official song of the National Association for the Advancement of Colored People (NAACP).

By 1905, Johnson was pursuing other interests besides music. He was serving as president of New York's Colored Republican Club and was taking courses in literature at Columbia University. One of his professors encouraged him to write about the lives of black Americans, and Johnson began work on a novel. Eventually published in 1912 as *The Autobiography of an Ex-Colored Man*, Johnson's first book strongly influenced the writers who took part in the Harlem Renaissance during the 1920s.

In the spring of 1906, Johnson decided to end his collaboration with Cole and the Johnson Brothers, and pursue a career that would be of greater service to his race. Through contacts in the Colored Republican Club, he received a diplomatic appointment as U.S. consul in Puerto Cabello, Venezuela, and served there for three years. In 1909, he was promoted to a more important diplomatic post in Corinto, Nicaragua. He performed his duties skillfully, hoping that he would eventually be transferred to a post in Europe.

When the Democratic party came to power in 1912, Johnson realized that his chances for promotion were slim. The following year, he resigned from the diplomatic corps and returned to Jacksonville with his wife, Grace. They had married three years earlier, after a lengthy courtship.

For a year, the 42-year-old Johnson tried to decide what line of work to pursue next. In late 1914, he and his wife moved to Harlem, which was in the midst of becoming the center of New York City's black community, and he became an editorial columnist for the *New York Age*, a leading black weekly newspaper. Over the next 10 years, he penned a number of editorials that sought to reverse the lowly status of black Americans.

Johnson's interest in black affairs soon led to his involvement with the recently founded NAACP. He began attending NAACP meetings in 1916 and was promptly elected vice-president of the local branch. That August, he even traveled to Amenia, New York, for an NAACP-sponsored black rights conference attended by more than 50 of the nation's most prominent black leaders. In the fight for black rights, Johnson's star was clearly rising.

It did not take long for him to impress the NAACP's leaders. In December 1916, Johnson was named the association's field secretary. His duties included traveling throughout the country on behalf of the organization, setting up new branches and recruiting new members. After three years of tireless effort, he had helped the NAACP to grow from 70 to 310 branches and its membership to increase from 9,000 to 100,000 members.

During America's participation in World War I, Johnson also served as the NAACP's acting executive secretary, the association's top position. In this role, he investigated acts of racial violence, led protests against lynching, and coordinated the NAACP's legal assistance for black defendants and funding for the homeless. He returned to his duties as field secretary in the spring of 1918 and recruited additional blacks to serve on the NAACP executive board, including Walter White, who became his chief assistant and was put in charge of investigating lynching cases.

In November 1920, Johnson was officially installed as the new executive secretary. During his 10 years in office, he skillfully coordinated the efforts of an underfinanced organization and an overworked staff. He relentlessly lobbied Congress for passage of antilynching legislation and led the NAACP in bringing suit against school boards to increase funding for black education. He also sponsored successful lawsuits to end housing discrimination, helped guarantee black voting rights in Texas, and supported labor organizer A. Philip Randolph's efforts to create a union of railway sleeping car porters.

Johnson's schedule became more and more taxing, and in 1929 he fell ill from exhaustion. He resigned as executive secretary in December 1930 to become professor of literature at Fisk University. He had maintained his literary interests while he worked at the NAACP: his books published in the 1920s were *The Book of American Negro Poetry* (1922), *The Book of American Negro Spirituals* (1925), and a collection of his own poetry, *God's Trombones* (1927). *Black Manhattan* (1930), an account of the Harlem Renaissance; his autobiography, *Along This Way* (1933); and *American Negroes: What Now?* (1934) were his final publications.

In his last years, Johnson and his wife divided their time between the Fisk campus, an apartment in Harlem, and a summer home in Massachusetts. He was driving in a heavy rainstorm in Maine on June 26, 1938, when a train struck his car at a railroad crossing. The collision instantly killed the 67-year-old James Weldon Johnson, who had devoted his life to racial equality so completely and in so many different ways.

MARTIN LUTHER KING, JR.

Civil rights leader Martin Luther King, Jr., was born on January 15, 1929, in Atlanta, Georgia. His father, Martin Luther King, Sr., was pastor of the Ebenezer Baptist Church, a leading black congregation in the city. His mother, Alberta Williams King, was the daughter of a former pastor of Ebenezer Baptist Church. Martin, Jr., his brother, Alfred, and sister, Willie Christine, grew up, as their parents and grandparents had, in the segregated South, where blacks learned about racial discrimination at an early age.

The warmth and support of his family and his father's church strengthened King while he was growing up. Friends and relatives recall that he was a normal boy who enjoyed sports, liked to read, and occasionally played pranks, which were promptly punished by his stern father.

After King graduated from high school in 1944, he entered Atlanta's Morehouse College, an all-male, all-black school. His parents had assumed that he would study for the ministry, but King was puzzled by "the emotionalism of Negro religion, the shouting and the stomping" that he saw in his father's church. "I didn't understand it," he said, "and it embarrassed me."

King changed his mind after hearing Morehouse College president Benjamin Mays preach. A Baptist minister, Mays was quiet and dignified, and from his pulpit in the college chapel he called for the black church to put aside some of its religious fundamentalism and lead the protest for social change. In February 1948, the 19-year-old King was ordained a minister and made assistant pastor at Ebenezer. He graduated from Morehouse several months later.

King's next stop was Crozer Seminary, near Philadelphia, to earn a degree in theology. Crozer presented a new world to him: nearly all its students were white. But by the end of his first year, he had become one of the most popular students at the seminary. His excellent grades also showed him to be among the brightest.

Meanwhile, King was developing a personal philosophy that would burn inside him for the rest of his life. A lecture on Indian leader Mahatma Gandhi provided the spark. Unique among political leaders, Gandhi stressed the power of love and nonviolent resistance as a means for changing people's opinions. Deeply impressed by this concept of peaceful defiance, King saw it as a way that black Americans might be able to break the shackles of segregation.

King received his bachelor's degree from Crozer in 1951, graduating at the top of his class. He was then awarded a scholarship to the School of Theology at Boston University. By the middle of his first year in Boston, he had met the woman who would become his wife: Coretta Scott, an Alabama native and an Antioch College graduate who was studying voice at the New England Conservatory of Music. They were married in June 1953 and had four children.

In the spring of 1954, after completing his classes for a doctorate, King was hired as the pastor of the Dexter Avenue Baptist Church in Montgomery, Alabama. He could not have chosen a more segregated city in the nation. Most of its black residents lived in ramshackle houses that did not have electricity or running water. Whites governed the city with an iron fist.

To King, the blacks of Montgomery seemed resigned to their fate. But change was coming: in May 1954, only a few months before his arrival, the U.S. Supreme Court had struck a severe blow against segregation. In its decision in the landmark case of *Brown v. Board of Education*, the Supreme Court declared that segregating school children by race was illegal.

Throughout the South, angry whites vowed to ignore the Supreme Court ruling. King responded by encouraging his parishioners to join the country's leading civil rights organization, the National Association for the Advancement of Colored People (NAACP). He also called on them to exercise their right to vote.

The battle for racial equality in Montgomery began in earnest on December 1, 1955, when Rosa Parks, a black seamstress, refused to obey a city ordinance that she give up her bus seat to a white passenger. She was arrested and jailed; in protest, the NAACP orchestrated a boycott of the city buses. The city's black pastors, including King, endorsed the protest, and the Montgomery bus boycott was born, with King hand-picked as the leader.

King's message of nonviolent resistance soon reached an audience that stretched far beyond Montgomery. By late 1956, the boycott had led to the desegregation of the city's buses, and King had emerged as a leading spokesman for civil rights. He took advantage of his growing fame in 1957 by organizing a public demonstration in Washington, D.C., to encourage congressional approval of a civil rights bill, the first of the 20th century. Held at the Lincoln Memorial on May 17, the Prayer Pilgrimage for Freedom attracted a crowd of 25,000 people and stamped King as the nation's most influential black leader.

To help spread the message of nonviolent resistance across America, King conferred with leading black clergymen and formed a new and powerful civil rights organization, the Southern Christian Leadership Conference (SCLC). As head of the Atlanta-based SCLC, he conducted a persistent campaign of nonviolent social protest, including sit-ins, interstate bus rides, and voter registration drives. Arrests and death threats did not deter him; he continued to inspire his supporters to fight for racial equality.

King took on all comers. In Birmingham, Alabama, a fortress of white supremacy, he began demanding that public facilities be desegregated. By the time his clash with city officials had ended in mid-1963, the local police's brutal handling of King and his demonstrators had shocked the entire nation and had resulted in a settlement in Birmingham.

Nowhere did King reach a larger audience than during his speech at the March on Washington for Jobs and Freedom, held in the nation's capital on August 28, 1963. Nearly 250,000 civil rights marchers gathered at the Lincoln Memorial to hear him proclaim at the end of the day-long demonstration, "I still have a dream. It is a dream deeply rooted in the American dream." His dream of a just society seemed all the more possible after he and his legions of supporters helped bring about the passage of the landmark Civil Rights Act of 1964, which made segregation a federal crime.

In honor of his peaceful efforts to end segregation, King earned the 1964 Nobel Peace Prize. At age 35, he was the youngest recipient in history.

The award was soon followed by additional political action. In 1965, he spearheaded a voting rights campaign in Selma, Alabama, that state troopers did their best to stamp out; yet their vicious thrashing of the protesters served only to speed the passage of voting rights legislation. In 1966, he launched the Chicago Freedom Movement, an attempt to win civil rights for urban blacks, and another voter registration march, the James Meredith March Against Fear. In 1967, he again took a stand against violence by publicly proclaiming his opposition to the Vietnam War.

Sadly for King, his message of nonviolence seemed to be doing little good by the middle of 1967. The Vietnam War was escalating, and America's black ghettos, filled with frustration over the slow pace of change, were exploding in violence.

In response, King began a new effort, the Poor People's Campaign, to call attention to the desperate need for economic justice. He called for another march on Washington, D.C., this time to bring thousands of the impoverished to the nation's capital. There, in direct sight of the Capitol, they would build a poor people's city of shacks and tents and shame Congress into aiding the poor.

In the middle of his planning for the Poor People's Campaign, King traveled to Memphis, Tennessee, in support of the city's striking garbage collectors. He addressed the congregation at Mason Temple on the night of April 3, 1968, returned to his room at the Lorraine Motel, and spent all of the next afternoon organizing the march supporting the garbage collectors. At precisely six o'clock, as King stood on the motel's balcony to head off to dinner, he was felled by assassin James Earl Ray's bullet.

Martin Luther King, Jr., was just 39 years old at the time of his death. But his vision of a prejudice-free society—the greatest of all American dreams—will endure forever.

MALCOLM X

Racial spokesman Malcolm X was born Malcolm Little on May 19, 1925, in Omaha, Nebraska. The fourth of Earl and Louise Little's eight children, he entered a world full of violence and fear.

Only a few weeks before Malcolm's birth, his father narrowly escaped being lynched by the nation's most notorious white supremacist group, the Ku Klux Klan.

Earl Little was an outspoken Baptist preacher from Georgia who had grown up surrounded by racial violence and had become a fierce opponent of discrimination. The Klan had targeted him because he had emerged as a spokesman for the Universal Negro Improvement Association (UNIA), founded by black nationalist leader Marcus Garvey to heighten black pride and promote black rights.

When Malcolm was still an infant, the Littles moved to the Midwest, finally settling in East Lansing, Michigan. There Earl Little eked out a living as the Great Depression spread across the nation. He also continued his black activist work for the UNIA, until a bitter day in 1931, when he was found beaten and run over by a trolley car. His murderers, most likely a white lynch mob, were never found.

In the aftermath of her husband's death, Louise Little struggled to support her children and finally went on welfare. Continually confronted with his family's poverty, Malcolm began to drift away from home. Occasionally he was caught performing petty criminal acts. When his mother suffered a breakdown and was committed to a mental hospital in 1937, he became a ward of the state and was placed in a foster home. A short time later, 13-year-old Malcolm Little was put in a juvenile detention center.

In school, Little encountered few problems. He ranked third in his junior high school class and was popular enough to be elected student body vice-president by his predominantly white classmates. But the die was already cast. Deep down, he did not feel accepted in the white world.

Little welcomed the change of scenery that accompanied his half-sister Ella's invitation to spend the summer of 1939 at her well-to-do home in Roxbury, a largely black section of Boston. There he learned what life was like for privileged blacks. He returned to the city the following spring and moved in with Ella.

Having little confidence that his schooling would lead to any sort of bright future, Little decided to go to work instead of continuing his education. His first job was as a shoe shiner at the Roseland State Ballroom, one of Boston's most popular dance halls. He supplemented his income by selling marijuana to some of the customers; and as the days passed, he became increasingly involved in the world of drugs, drinking, and gambling. The more spending money he had in his pockets, it seemed, the more his appetite for vices grew.

At the end of 1941, Little moved to the Harlem district of New York City and was soon drawn into the black community's underworld of hustlers and thieves. He became known on the streets as a drug peddler, Detroit Red.

Little thrived for a while as a hustler. Then the police began to watch him closely, forcing him to find another way to obtain money. He turned to armed robbery and numbers running.

Scrapes with rival hustlers sent Little back to Boston, where his criminal past finally caught up with him. The police hauled him from the streets, and in February 1946 he was sentenced to 10 years in prison. At first, he remained a wildly angry, antisocial young man who took great pride in being an outcast. But as his prison term wore on, he began to listen to three of his siblings as they encouraged him to embrace the black separatist religious movement known as the Nation of Islam, with its message of black superiority and resistance to white domination.

The Nation sought to instill racial pride and promote self-sufficiency while offering its legions of disciples, particularly the black urban poor, a sense of mission in life. Elijah Muhammad, the head of the Nation, and his followers, known as Black Muslims, claimed that all whites were devils who were about to fall from their positions of power. In their place would rise the black community.

As Little learned more about Muhammad, he saw parallels between the Black Muslim leader's work and his own father's social activism. In 1949, Little wrote a long letter to Muhammad and was welcomed into the sect. In keeping with the Nation's custom, Malcolm Little replaced his surname with the letter *X*.

Malcolm X was paroled from prison in 1952 and immediately set out on a mission to use the teachings of the Nation of Islam "to stir and wake and resurrect the black man." His blistering attacks on America's long-standing racial attitudes and his success in recruiting new members—in pool halls, barrooms, and on street corners—soon established him as the ministry's chief operative. A spellbinding public speaker, he urged his fellow blacks to battle racial oppression with militant action.

In June 1954, as a reward for his hard work, Malcolm X was appointed the head of Temple Number Seven in Harlem. Its membership grew swiftly, and during the rest of the decade he organized new temples in cities along the East and West Coasts, drawing converts from the more prosperous and educated middle class. Members were required to make monetary contributions to the Nation, which began buying real estate and starting small businesses. Profits from these ventures enabled the Nation to expand greatly.

At the same time that the number of Black Muslims was growing, the Reverend Martin Luther King, Jr., and other civil rights leaders were challenging racial segregation in the South by holding nonviolent protests. Malcolm X had nothing but contempt for their passive approach to the problems facing black society. He began spreading his message of revolt to crowds in the northern ghettos, telling his listeners that they could not afford to wait any longer for racial justice to be won.

By the early 1960s, Malcolm X and the Nation of Islam had become well known to both whites and blacks throughout the United States. Critics charged that he was a hatemonger who preached violence and destruction. He replied that only radical tactics would cure America's racial problems. "Yes, I'm an extremist," he said. "The black race here in North America is in extremely bad condition."

In 1962, the ailing Elijah Muhammad asked Malcolm X to represent him in public. These appearances aroused the jealousy of other Black Muslims, who attempted to turn the older man against his protégé by spreading rumors that he was trying to usurp Muhammad's power.

Before long, a serious rift developed between Malcolm X and Muhammad. Following President John F.

Kennedy's assassination in November 1963, Malcolm X declared that "the chickens [have] come home to roost," meaning that whites were being repaid for creating a climate of violence in America. This time, Malcolm X had gone too far. The comment created an uproar throughout the United States and provided Muhammad with an opportunity to deal with the supposed threat to his own leadership. He promptly suspended Malcolm X from his duties for 90 days.

Toward the end of his suspension, Malcolm X learned that a high-ranking Black Muslim had instructed that the fiery, 38-year-old minister be killed. Malcolm X responded by announcing in March 1964 that he was leaving the Nation to form Muslim Mosque, Incorporated, an organization to push for black self-determination. Less than a month later, he embarked on a spiritual pilgrimage to Mecca, the Islamic holy city, where he was embraced by Muslims of every race. A doctrine of black supremacy, he saw, was not part of traditional Islam.

It was a changed Malcolm X who returned to the United States in May 1964—though still a militant leader, he was now willing to work with civil rights organizations to build a better way of life for blacks. To help achieve this goal on a world-wide scale, he founded a nonreligious branch of Muslim Mosque, the Organization of Afro-American Unity (OAAU). But his renewed effort to break the shackles of white supremacy made him the target of death threats. He assumed his rivals in the Nation were behind the warnings.

On the night of February 13, 1965, Malcolm X's home in East Elmhurst, New York, was firebombed; he and his family barely managed to escape from the flaming house. Then, barely a week later, on February 21, during a rally at the Audubon Ballroom in Harlem, three gunmen—allegedly Black Muslims—shot him dead. His New York City headquarters was burned down two days after the shooting. In the wake of Malcolm X's death would remain his call for sweeping changes in American society.

THURGOOD MARSHALL

The United States Supreme Court justice Thurgood Marshall was born on July 2, 1908, in West Baltimore, Maryland. He was the second son of William, a waiter, and Norma Marshall, a schoolteacher. William Marshall, who had little education but a keen mind, taught young Thurgood how to debate and encouraged him to pursue a legal career. From his mother, Thurgood learned tact and diplomacy. The Marshalls stressed the value of personal dignity and modesty, but they never recommended meekness. "Anyone calls you nigger," said William to Thurgood, "you not only got my permission to fight him—you got my orders to fight him."

Graduating from high school in 1925, Marshall enrolled in Lincoln University, an all-black Philadelphia institution where he became a star debater. In the fall of his senior year, Marshall married University of Pennsylvania student Vivian Burey; the following June, he graduated from Lincoln with honors in the humanities. He entered the law school of Howard University, a black institution in Washington, D.C., in 1930.

At the end of his first year, Howard's professors named Marshall top student in his class. Among the distinguished professors who helped him polish his skills was Charles Hamilton Houston, a brilliant attorney and pioneering civil rights activist. Houston provided legal assistance to the National Association for the Advancement of Colored People (NAACP), an organization founded in 1909 to combat racial discrimination. Marshall often helped him plan strategy for his NAACP cases.

In 1933, Marshall graduated first in his class from Howard Law School. Although Harvard University immediately offered him a postgraduate scholarship, he was eager to begin practicing law and turned it down. After passing the Maryland State law examination, he opened a law office in east Baltimore.

In the grip of the Great Depression (1929–40), few Americans of any race could afford legal representation, and black lawyers had a particularly hard time. In his first year of practice, Marshall had no paying clients, and he often took on the cases of poor people, thereby earning a reputation as "the little man's lawyer." Preparing for each trial with painstaking care, he won many of his early cases.

Marshall's public service work gained him not only experience but a steadily growing reputation. In 1934, the local chapter of the NAACP named him as its lawyer, an unpaid but exhilarating job. He kicked off his NAACP career by organizing a boycott of white-owned Baltimore stores that sold to blacks in a black neighborhood yet employed only whites. When the shopkeepers responded by suing the NAACP, Marshall teamed up with Charles Houston and successfully defended the organization in federal court.

In 1935, the NAACP began to concentrate on integrating graduate and professional schools. With Houston, Marshall scored his first major court victory when he won a suit against the University of Maryland for refusing to admit blacks to its law school. In 1936, Marshall accepted a job as assistant to Houston, who had become first special counsel at NAACP headquarters in New York City. Defending the rights of black students and teachers in the South, the two men spent the next two years traveling from one southern courthouse to another. Between trips, Marshall continued to help poor clients at his small Baltimore office.

Marshall's first case as assistant special counsel involved the University of Missouri Law School, which had refused to admit a qualified black student. Working with Houston, Marshall used the "separate-but-equal" doctrine in arguing the Missouri case, asserting that the law school had to admit the student unless it could offer "equal" education at an all-black institution. (U.S. courts had been using this doctrine, established by a Supreme Court case known as *Plessy v. Ferguson*, to decide segregation cases since 1896. Basically, *Plessy* allowed racial segregation as long as blacks had access to "equal" or equivalent facilities.)

The Missouri Law School case went all the way to the U.S. Supreme Court, which found in the NAACP's favor by a vote of six to two. The decision meant that Missouri—and other states—now had only two choices: to admit blacks to their all-white, publicly funded schools, or to build and staff brand-new, equal facilities for blacks—an almost impossibly expensive proposition. Elated NAACP officials realized that one day the Supreme Court might extend the doctrine to the nation's public schools at all levels.

In 1939, Marshall, now black America's most prominent attorney, became director-counsel of a new organization: the NAACP Legal Defense and Educational Fund, Inc., a body created to provide free legal aid to blacks who suffered racial injustice. As fund chief, Marshall prepared his first solo Supreme Court brief in 1940. In this case, *Chambers v. Florida*, the NAACP sought to overturn the convictions of three black men accused of murdering a white man. Marshall argued that police officials had wrung confessions from the men after five days of nonstop grilling, and that such "sunrise confessions" violated the U.S. Constitution's guarantee of "due process of law." The court agreed, giving Marshall a major victory.

Marshall next focused his sights on a notorious device employed to keep southern blacks from voting.

In the South, primary winners almost always won the election. Only party members could vote in the primary, and only whites could belong to the party. Marshall based his 1944 challenge to the "white primary" on the Fifteenth Amendment, which forbids states to deprive citizens of their vote "on account of race, color, or previous condition of servitude." The U.S. Supreme Court upheld Marshall's argument, a decision that sounded the death knell for the South's white primary.

In 1946, the NAACP awarded Marshall its highest award, the Spingarn Medal. By 1948, the 40-year-old lawyer had earned the nickname "Mr. Civil Rights." That same year, he went after unfair housing practices. Arguing before the Supreme Court, Marshall maintained that restrictive covenants—agreements between whites that effectively kept blacks out of white neighborhoods—restricted blacks' rights as Americans. Agreeing, the court struck down the covenants. Two years later Marshall argued and won two major segregation-in-education cases before the Supreme Court. His twin victories led to the admission of black students to the Universities of Oklahoma and Texas, and in 1950 he succeeded in getting a black law student enrolled at Louisiana State University.

In 1952, Marshall and his NAACP legal team scored one of the organization's most resounding triumphs. After extensive preparation, the lawyers brought *Brown v. Board of Education of Topeka* to the Supreme Court. A combination of five cases from around the country, *Brown* was aimed at a formidable target: public school segregation in America. Marshall argued that segregation was inherently unequal because it implied that government believed "Negroes [to be] inferior to all other human beings," and that it had a permanent, devastating effect on black children. In May 1954, a year and a half after he began his battle for Brown, Marshall had the joy of hearing Chief Justice Earl Warren read the Supreme Court's unanimous verdict: "In the field of public education the doctrine of 'separate but equal' has no place." School segregation had been declared unconstitutional.

Marshall's victory was marred by the news that his wife was fatally ill with cancer. Following her death in 1955, Marshall married a Hawaiian, Cecelia Suyat, with whom he eventually had two sons. During the seven years that followed his marriage, he waged scores of civil rights battles, fighting southern efforts to escape school desegregation, opposing southern attempts to ban the NAACP, lining up his forces to back the Reverend Martin Luther King, Jr., and vigorously defending civil rights demonstrators.

In September 1962, President John F. Kennedy appointed Marshall to the Second Circuit Court of Appeals. During his four years as a judge, Marshall ruled on a variety of cases, including the use of illegally obtained evidence in criminal trials, the deportation of aliens, and the First Amendment right to free expression. Not one of his 98 majority opinions was overturned by the Supreme Court. This remarkable record was in large part responsible for Marshall's 1965 appointment as U.S. solicitor general, a post never before held by a black citizen. During his two years as the nation's top-ranking courtroom advocate, Marshall won 14 of his 19 cases, most of them dealing with civil rights and privacy issues.

In 1967, Thurgood Marshall again made history when President Lyndon B. Johnson named him America's first black Supreme Court justice. In case after case, he defended individual rights and educational and legal equality for all races. After more than two decades of distinguished service as an Associate Justice, Marshall retired from the court in 1991.

Two years later, on January 24, 1993, Marshall died of heart failure at Bethesda Naval Medical Center in Maryland. He was 84 years old.

At Marshall's funeral service, Chief Justice William H. Rehnquist said in his eulogy: "As a result of his career as a lawyer and as a judge, Thurgood Marshall left an indelible mark not just upon the law but upon his country. Inscribed above the front entrance to the Supreme Court building are the words 'Equal justice under law.' Surely no one individual did more to make these words a reality than Thurgood Marshall."

ADAM CLAYTON POWELL, JR.

$\mathbf{P}$olitical leader Adam Clayton Powell, Jr., was born on November 29, 1908, in New Haven, Connecticut. Shortly after his birth, he and his older sister, Blanche, moved with their parents, Mattie and the Reverend Adam Clayton Powell, Sr., to Harlem, the New York City district that was just emerging as the nation's largest black community.

A Baptist minister, the senior Powell became pastor of the century-old Abyssinian Baptist Church in midtown. He immediately set to work revitalizing it by increasing the church's membership and improving its financial resources. With the help of local reformers, the dynamic Powell also made the church a center for the entire black community. It fed the poor, offered recreation to the young, and presented musical and dramatic performances.

As the influential pastor's son, Adam, Jr., enjoyed a privileged upbringing. He lived in a spacious brownstone and, being the baby of the family, was constantly pampered, especially by his mother. Gradually, he emerged from her shadow.

Fair skinned with straight black hair, Powell could, in the phrase of the day, "pass for white." But his father, being an advocate of black pride, made sure that Adam, Jr., understood his roots. And when his son was 14 years old, the senior Powell moved his church uptown, to a new building in the heart of Harlem.

The Abyssinian Baptist Church thrived in its new location. The congregation grew to more than 10,000 members, the largest of any Protestant church in America. Adam, Jr., the reverend hoped, would one day preside over the church.

The younger Powell was a good student in elementary school. But he saw his grades drop almost as soon as he entered Townsend Harris High School. Fancying himself a ladies' man, he led an active social life. Prodded by his father, he enrolled at the City College of New York in 1925, only to flunk out of school that spring. A busy social calendar was not the only reason for this lapse: his sister died after an operation that March, leaving him devastated.

In the fall, Powell tried college once again. He attended Colgate University, studied reasonably hard, and graduated in 1930. He promptly became assistant minister and business manager of the Abyssinian and also entered Columbia University's Teachers College, from which he received a master's degree in religious studies in 1932. The next year, he married singer Isabel Washington.

By then, Powell had thrown himself completely into his work. Seeing the Great Depression leave an alarming number of Harlemites without jobs, he launched a campaign to help the local black community. He proved to be an extremely capable leader, organizing boycotts and pickets to combat the racial discrimination and despair that plagued Harlem. "My father said he built the church and I would interpret it. This I made up my mind to do," he said. "I intended to fashion that church into a mighty weapon, keen-edged and sharp-pointed."

In 1937, the 29-year-old Powell succeeded his father as the Abyssinian's minister. He used his position as the nation's best-known and most influential black clergyman as a springboard to political office. In 1941, he ran as an independent candidate for a seat on the New York City Council. "I am not seeking a political job," he claimed. "I am fighting for the chance to give my people the best representation in the affairs of their city, to help make Harlem the number one community of New York."

That November, New York's voters made him the first black city councilman ever.

In 1943, Powell decided to go after a larger political prize. The U.S. Congress had recently created a new congressional district in Harlem, and Powell announced his intention to run for the seat as a Democrat. The following year, he was elected to Congress by an overwhelming majority and thus became the first U.S. congressman to represent the district of Harlem.

Soon after taking his seat in the House of Representatives, Powell divorced his wife Isabel and married Hazel Scott, a well-known jazz pianist and singer. They had one child, Adam Clayton Powell III, who was born in 1946. (Powell was married for a third time in 1960, to Puerto Rican native Yvette Marjorie Flores Diago; their son, Adam Clayton Powell IV, was born in 1962.)

As a congressman, Powell quickly established a reputation as a militant, uncompromising champion of black rights. He became especially noted for attacking southern congressmen who supported segregation. In 1945, he even went so far as to publish *Marching Blacks*, a book that urged southern blacks to move north, where they would find greater economic opportunities and be allowed to vote, a right often denied them in the South.

Powell was nothing if not politically independent and disdainful of congressional protocol, and his crusade to foster black rights wore thin on many of his colleagues. One of the things that annoyed them the most was his constant use of what came to be known as the Powell amendment. He employed this legislative tactic for the first time in 1946, when he attached to a bill an amendment that denied federal money to any state that excluded black schoolchildren from its food fund program. The bill—with its attached Powell amendment—was passed.

After that, Powell decided to try to repeat his success. As a member of the House Education and Labor Committee, he attached an amendment to nearly every education bill that denied federal funds to any state that practiced segregation. He carried this practice well into the 1960s, as the South continued to resist every attempt to integrate its schools. Southern congressmen refused to support any bill that included the Powell amendment, and without their votes, federal aid to education suffered. Powell, however, maintained that making use of the Powell amendment was one of the best ways a black politician could agitate for black rights.

As a leader in the fight against segregation and an irritant to the powerbrokers in Congress, Powell was beloved by his constituents. He fought for new social welfare programs and, as chairman of the House Education and Labor Committee in the 1960s, he helped guide important civil rights bills through Congress. He was a pioneer in fostering black solidarity.

But the early 1960s, a number of dark clouds had already begun to appear on Powell's horizon. The Justice Department and the Internal Revenue Service had begun digging into his affairs a decade earlier, and in 1958 he had been indicted for tax evasion. His case was dismissed when it was brought to trial two years later, but the storm was still brewing.

It finally broke in 1967, at the tail end of a House committee's investigation of Powell's congressional payroll. It was revealed that he was paying salaries to his wife Yvette, his companion Corinne Huff, and several other nongovernment people. And he had been illegally spending the taxpayers' money in a host of other ways.

Armed with the investigative committee's findings on Powell's misconduct, the House of Representatives voted on his fate. The verdict was overwhelmingly against him. Twenty-three years after he was first voted into Congress, Powell was stripped of his congressional seat by his fellow representatives. He immediately appealed the decision in the courts.

Meanwhile, a special election was held in April 1967 to fill Powell's now-vacant seat in Congress. The Harlem voters reelected him, and then handed him a 13th term in the 1968 elections.

Back in Congress, Powell was fined $25,000 by his colleagues, who also took away his seniority. His spirits picked up somewhat half a year later, when the U.S. Supreme Court ruled in favor of his appeal, declaring that "the House was without power to exclude him from membership." But the summer of 1969 was hardly a time for celebration. His doctors had just informed him that he was seriously ill with cancer.

Throughout the following year, Powell hardly spent any time at all answering the congressional roll call. And when the Democratic primary for Congress was held in June 1970, Harlem turned against him for the first time. His political career was over.

Powell's life came to an end on April 4, 1972, following an emergency operation in Miami. His body was returned to Harlem for a funeral service at the Abyssinian Baptist Church, where his remarkable career as a crusader for black rights began.

ASA PHILIP RANDOLPH

Labor leader Asa Philip Randolph was born on April 15, 1889, in Crescent City, Florida. His family moved north to Jacksonville when he was two years old, and it was there that he spent the rest of his childhood.

Asa and his older brother, James, were taught by their parents, Elizabeth and James Randolph, Sr., to be proud and independent, to stand up to racial discrimination, and to help the needy. Their father was a minister in the African Methodist Episcopal (AME) church and led a small congregation. He also preached to blacks in rural communities near the city.

Jacksonville at the time was one of the most integrated towns in the South. But as Randolph grew older, instances of racial violence began to increase, until tensions heightened following a fire in 1901 that destroyed two-thirds of the city and led to scenes of looting. The crimes were attributed to blacks, and laws were passed to enforce segregation and to deprive blacks of the positions of authority they held. The Reverend James Randolph promptly forbade his sons from using any segregated public facilities, including the streetcars and the library.

A solid student, Randolph enrolled in Jacksonville's Cookman Institute when he was 14 years old. There he shone in the choir and on the baseball team. He graduated in 1907 as the head of his class and delivered a valedictory address on racial pride.

Lacking the money to go to college, Randolph held a variety of jobs. All the while, he resolved to fight in some way for the improvement of conditions for black Americans. He had already decided not to follow in his father's footsteps and become a minister, but he did have a strong social conscience.

In 1911, shortly after celebrating his 22nd birthday, Randolph left Jacksonville and moved to New York City, settling in the Harlem district. During the next three years, he worked at a series of low-paying jobs: telephone switchboard operator, dishwasher, floor scrubber, porter. He divided his spare time between the public library, a discussion group at a local

Methodist church, and night classes at the City College of New York, where he studied public speaking and social sciences.

Randolph's studies led him to the writings of Karl Marx, the German political philosopher who advocated a society in which everything is owned and controlled by the state. Randolph believed that Marx's socialist system provided the best means for achieving greater racial equality in America. Because most blacks belonged to the working class, they had much to gain in a society in which there was no such thing as private property.

Randolph made his first inroads into labor organization while at City College. He formed a discussion group, the Independent Political Council, that supported the American labor movement and its demands for higher wages and better working conditions. Through this group, he wound up meeting Lucille Campbell Green. The two were married in 1914 and spent nearly 50 years together.

Shortly after his marriage, Randolph befriended Chandler Owen, a Columbia University sociology student who also believed strongly in socialism. Together, they stopped attending classes, joined the Socialist party, and took to the streets of Harlem, becoming streetcorner orators preaching social reform. They soon attracted the attention of William White, who invited them in 1917 to edit a magazine, the *Hotel Messenger*, intended for black waiters working in the city's hotels.

The venture came to an end seven months later, but by then the two men had ideas for a new magazine that would serve as a voice for black workers. The first issue was published in November 1917, and Randolph and Owen called it *The Messenger*, subtitling it the "only radical Negro magazine in America." Published monthly, it quickly gained a prominent place among New York's political journals, being considered among the most intellectual and the most controversial. The editorials called for cooperation among workers of all races and for a relentless assault on racism. Above all, it promoted racial pride.

"We were young, we were against everything, and we weren't going to back down from anything," Randolph said of his early days with *The Messenger*. And he was true to his word. He argued that black Americans should not fight in World War I so long as they were being subjected to racially discriminatory laws. He said that blacks should use arms, if necessary, to defend themselves. He was also outspokenly critical of black nationalist leader Marcus Garvey as well as more mainstream black leaders, such as Booker T. Washington and W. E. B. Du Bois, claiming that their policies encouraged blacks to patiently accept oppression. By 1919, the U.S. State Department had declared Randolph "the most dangerous Negro in America."

The labor movement remained one of Randolph's greatest passions. He wrote many editorials criticizing the American Federation of Labor (AFL), the labor unions' governing body, because blacks were excluded from its unions. But by the mid-1920s he finally had to admit to himself that neither the AFL nor the Socialist party was interested in helping black workers. Discouraged, he quit the Socialist party and decided to take matters into his own hands.

In 1925, Randolph was asked to organize the porters of the Pullman Company, which owned and operated the sleeping cars used on long-distance passenger routes, into the Brotherhood of Sleeping Car Porters. All of the company's porters were black, underpaid, and overworked. During the months that followed, Randolph and several associates traveled around the country establishing branches of the union. By the end of 1926, it claimed a membership of nearly 6,000— more than half the number of porters who worked for the Pullman Company.

It took 12 long years for the Randolph-led Brotherhood of Sleeping Car Porters to win the battle for better working conditions. But on August 25, 1937, when a labor pact was finally reached with the company, giving the porters the wage and work-hour concessions they had demanded, the union became the first group of blacks to sign a labor agreement with a major corporation.

Randolph's triumph elevated him to national prominence and labeled him the leader of America's black community. He tried to use his newly won influence to integrate all of the AFL's unions and to end the nation's racially segregated armed forces, but nothing seemed to work. In 1941, he began to organize a massive protest march on Washington, D.C., to "shake up America." He said that the "leaders in Washington will never give the Negro justice until they see masses—10, 20, 50 thousand Negroes on the White House Lawn!"

The threat of the march on Washington brought about the end of racially discriminatory employment policies in the defense industry and the federal government. In 1948, Randolph's lobbying brought about the desegregation of the armed forces and the creation of a Fair Employment Board to eliminate racial discrimination in government agencies.

By the 1950s, the labor movement finally began to accept the principles that Randolph had been championing for decades, and more and more unions became integrated. In 1955, when the AFL merged with the other leading labor federation, the Congress of Industrial Organizations (CIO), Randolph was elected to the newly formed AFL-CIO's executive council. Two years later, he was voted in as the federation's vice-president.

A tireless champion of the working man, Randolph carried on his fight into the 1960s, helping to form the Negro American Labor Council, which sought to increase the role of blacks in labor unions, and serving as its president. And he remained a guiding light of the nation's civil rights movement. In 1963, he again issued the call for a march on Washington. This time the march took place on August 28, and the massive demonstration, called the March on Washington for Jobs and Freedom, proved to be the crowning event of the civil rights effort, highlighted by the Reverend Martin Luther King, Jr.'s "I Have a Dream" speech. Less than a year later, President Lyndon B. Johnson awarded Randolph the Medal of Freedom for his service to his country.

Randolph continued as president of the Brotherhood of Sleeping Car Porters until 1968. He died 11 years later, on May 16, barely a month after his 90th birthday. His passing recalled the words of journalist Murray Kempton, who said, "It is hard to make anyone who has never met him believe that A. Philip Randolph must be the greatest man who has lived in the United States in this century. But it is harder yet to make anyone who has ever known him believe anything else."

WALTER WHITE

Civil rights leader Walter Francis White was born on July 1, 1893, in Atlanta, Georgia. His father, George White, was a mailman; his mother, Madeline, was a former schoolteacher. Walter and his six brothers and sisters grew up in a two-story house that stood on the border between the city's black and white communities.

The Whites' light skin color also put them on a border of sorts. Although they considered themselves black, they could have easily passed for white, which they refused to do.

The White children were taught to regard friends, family, and faith more highly than material possessions. Education was deeply prized, and Walter's early interest in learning was encouraged by both parents. He constantly borrowed books from the library at the church he attended. And every day after school, he rode with his father on his mail route and engaged in long-running debates. Whenever Walter's knowledge seemed hazy on a subject, George White sent him to the church library to learn more about it.

One night in September 1906, racial hatred erupted in Atlanta, with white mobs attacking blacks. The Whites were initially spared from the violence because they were not recognized as being black. But a mob marched toward their street on the second night of the riot. Only a volley of gunfire from neighbors saved the family from harm.

The incident left a deep impression on Walter White. "I knew who I was," he said. "I was a Negro, a human being with an invisible pigmentation which marked me a person to be hunted, hanged, abused, discriminated against."

To rise above his station in life, White chose to excel. He graduated from high school in 1912 and enrolled at Atlanta University. There he played football, won awards for his debating skills, and was elected president of his class. Upon graduating in 1916, he went to work for an insurance company.

Meanwhile, a city government plan to limit black children to a sixth-grade education attracted White's attention. He and a number of Atlanta's educated blacks protested the proposal, arguing that the city had a legal obligation to provide equal schooling to blacks and whites. The plan was scrapped, prompting White and his allies to press for improvements in the educational system. To marshal support, they formed a chapter of a new and growing civil rights organization, the National Association for the Advancement of Colored People (NAACP). White was elected the branch's secretary.

In 1918, White moved to New York City and became assistant secretary of the entire NAACP. One of the association's chief aims was to put a stop to the racial violence that was occurring throughout the United States, especially in the South. Between 1910 and 1920, almost 900 blacks died at the hands of lynch mobs.

One of White's first assignments was to investigate a lynching in Estill Springs, Tennessee. Letting local residents assume he was white, he tricked them into revealing the details of the murder, then returned to New York to publish the entire story. It received widespread attention and helped recruit many new members to the NAACP and its antilynching campaign.

White involved himself in a broad range of NAACP activities, including the ongoing battle to desegregate schools, hospitals, and neighborhoods. Lynchings and race riots, however, became his specialty. He traveled to Chicago in the summer of 1919 to investigate a series of riots. Then he headed to Phillips County,

Arkansas, where roving white mobs had massacred perhaps as many as 200 black sharecroppers. Posing as a northern newspaper reporter, White uncovered the truth about the killings.

In 1922, White married NAACP staff member Leah Gladys Powell, with whom he had two children: a daughter, Jane, and a son, Walter, Jr. The Whites became part of the social and intellectual life then thriving in Harlem, the black New York City district where they made their home. White himself contributed greatly to the black community's cultural life. By the end of the decade, he had published three books that brought him great acclaim: two novels, *The Fire in the Flint* (1924) and *Flight* (1926), and *Rope and Faggot*, a study of lynching in America.

White's literary successes did not slow him down. He continued his rigorous schedule of NAACP activities, traveling thousands of miles each year while serving as a major fundraiser for the association and continuing his investigations of racial injustice. All told, he personally investigated 41 lynchings and 8 race riots.

One of White's major battles began in 1930, when President Herbert Hoover named a circuit court judge from North Carolina, John J. Parker, to fill a vacancy on the U.S. Supreme Court. White investigated the judge's record and discovered that, in his unsuccessful bid to become governor in 1920, Parker had called for an end to black voting rights. White sent Parker a telegram, asking if he still held such a belief. When Parker failed to respond, White and the NAACP board of directors decided to oppose Parker's appointment.

First, the NAACP asked Hoover to withdraw his nomination. When the president refused, the association took the fight to the U.S. Senate, which must confirm all Supreme Court nominees, and then to cities around the nation. White testified against Parker before the Senate committee considering the appointment, then dispatched NAACP officials to the organization's regional branches to inform black voters of the threat Parker posed to their rights. The black community was encouraged to contact their senators and urge them to oppose Parker.

A flood of protest, in the form of letters, telegrams, petitions, telephone calls, and demonstrators, descended on Washington, D.C. Newspapers throughout the country debated the Parker appointment. On May 7, 1930, the voice of black America was heard. The Senate voted 41–39 to deny Parker a seat on the Supreme Court.

In 1931, White was rewarded for his hard work. James Weldon Johnson, who had served as the NAACP's executive secretary since 1920, stepped down from his post because of poor health. White was named to replace his mentor and close friend as the association's top official.

White had his work cut out for him as head of the NAACP. The Great Depression, the worst economic collapse in the country's history, was producing more social unrest and racial violence. After Franklin D. Roosevelt became president in 1932, White repeatedly urged the nation's leader to speak out in favor of antilynching legislation. Finally, in early 1934, Roosevelt delivered a radio address in which he denounced lynching as murder, and public support increased for a federal antilynching bill. Although Congress failed to pass legislation that outlawed lynching, White's relentless campaign steadily caused the grim practice to diminish.

White worked to ease racial tensions on all fronts. In 1943, when riots erupted in Detroit, his appeal to the president succeeded in bringing federal troops to the city to restore order. That same year, he helped bring calm to Harlem following an outbreak of violence.

In early 1944, White took a leave of absence from the NAACP to travel abroad as a correspondent during World War II and to observe the treatment of black servicemen serving in segregated combat units. For more than a year, he visited military installations in Europe, the Middle East, North Africa, and the Pacific, and sent back reports of racial discrimination.

Back home after the war ended in 1945, White served as a consultant to the American delegation at the founding meeting of the United Nations. Meanwhile, he discovered that outbreaks of violence directed against blacks were on the rise. In 1946, he worked with President Harry S. Truman to establish the Committee on Civil Rights, a group to investigate civil liberties violations. The committee's subsequent report called for sweeping reforms, including the passage of 27 civil rights acts.

In 1948, Truman sent Congress a massive program of civil rights legislation. Southern senators hastily defeated each measure. But the president would not be deterred. He issued two historic executive orders:

one of them desegregated the armed forces, the other called for all federal agencies to practice fair employment.

Truman's actions were crowning triumphs for White. The NAACP chief had spent decades championing greater legal protection of black rights. At last, he had succeeded in pushing a racist, segregated United States into an era of integrated education, housing, employment, military service, and public facilities.

White's achievement did not come without a price. In 1947, he suffered a heart attack and was forced to cut back on his busy schedule. His duties at the NAACP were reduced, and he devoted his last years to writing his autobiography, *A Man Called White* (1948), as well as an evaluation of the civil rights movement.

Walter White died of a heart attack on March 28, 1955, at the age of 61.

❧ FURTHER READING ☙

Jesse Jackson

Colton, Elizabeth. *The Jackson Phenomenon*. New York: Doubleday, 1989.

Jakoubek, Robert E. *Jesse Jackson*. New York: Chelsea House, 1991.

Landess, Thomas H. *Jesse Jackson and the Politics of Race*. Ottawa, IL: Jameson Books, 1985.

James Weldon Johnson

Fleming, Robert E. *James Weldon Johnson & Arna Wendell Bontemps*. G K Hall, 1987.

Johnson, James Weldon. *Negro Americans, What Now?* New York: AMS Press, 1971.

Tolbert-Rochaleau, Jane. *James Weldon Johnson*. New York: Chelsea House, 1988.

Martin Luther King, Jr.

Branch, Taylor. *Parting the Waters: America in the King Years 1954–63*. New York: Simon & Schuster, 1988.

Jakoubek, Robert. *Martin Luther King, Jr.* New York: Chelsea House, 1989.

King, Coretta Scott. *My Life with Martin Luther King, Jr.* New York: Holt, Rinehart & Winston, 1969.

Malcolm X

Davies, Mark. *Malcolm X*. Englewood Cliffs, NJ: Silver Burdett Press, 1990.

Gallen, David. *Malcolm X*. New York: Carroll & Graf, 1992.

Rummel, Jack. *Malcolm X*. New York: Chelsea House, 1989.

Thurgood Marshall

Aldred, Lisa. *Thurgood Marshall*. New York: Chelsea House, 1990.

Adam Clayton Powell, Jr.

Hamilton, Charles V. *Adam Clayton Powell, Jr.* New York: Atheneum, 1991.

Haskins, James. *Adam Clayton Powell: Portrait of a Marching Black*. New York: Dial Press, 1974.

Asa Philip Randolph

Anderson, Jervis. *A. Philip Randolph: A Biographical Portrait*. Berkeley: University of California Press, 1986.

Garfinkel, Herbert. *When Negroes March: The March on Washington Movement in the Organizational Politics for FEPC*. New York: Atheneum, 1969.

Hanley, Sally. *A. Philip Randolph*. New York: Chelsea House, 1989.

Walter White

Fraser, Jane. *Walter White*. New York: Chelsea House, 1991.

Waldron, Edward E. *Walter White and the Harlem Renaissance*. Port Washington, NY: Kennikat Press, 1978.

White, Walter. *How Far the Promised Land?* New York: Viking, 1955.

❧ Index ❧

Bevel, James, 8

Clinton, Bill, 11
Cole, Bob, 14

Du Bois, W. E. B., 50
Dukakis, Michael, 10

Farrakhan, Louis, 10

Gandhi, Mohandas K. (Mahatma), 21
Garvey, Marcus, 27, 50

Hoover, Herbert, 57, 58
Houston, Charles Hamilton, 34, 35
Hussein, Saddam, 10–11

Jackson, Charles, 6
Jackson, Helen Burns, 5–6
Jackson, Jacqueline Davis, 6–7
Jackson, Jesse, 5–11
Johnson, Agnes, 13
Johnson, Grace, 16
Johnson, Helen Dillet, 12–13
Johnson, James, Sr., 12–13
Johnson, James Weldon, 12–18, 58
Johnson, John Rosamond, 13
Johnson, Lyndon B., 7, 39, 52

Kempton, Murray, 52–53
Kennedy, John F., 30–31
King, Alberta Williams, 19
King, Alfred, 19
King, Coretta Scott, 21
King, Martin, Jr., 19
King, Martin Luther, Jr., 7, 19–25, 30,
    38, 52
King, Martin Luther, Sr., 19
King, Willie, 19

Little, Earl, 26
Little, Ella, 28
Little, Louise, 26

Malcolm X, 26–32
Marshall, Cecilia Suyat, 38
Marshall, Norma, 33
Marshall, Thurgood, 33–39
Marshall, Vivian Burey, 34
Marshall, William, 33–34
Mays, Benjamin, 20
Muhammad, Elijah, 29

Owen, Chandler, 49

Parker, John J., 57, 58
Parks, Rosa, 22
Powell, Adam Clayton, III, 43
Powell, Adam Clayton, Jr., 40–46
Powell, Adam Clayton, Sr., 40
Powell, Blanche, 40
Powell, Hazel Scott, 43
Powell, Isabel Washington, 42
Powell, Mattie, 40
Powell, Yvette 43, 45
Powell-Diago Adam Clayton, 43

Randolph, Asa Philip, 17, 47–53
Randolph, Elizabeth, 47
Randolph, James, 47–48
Randolph, James, Sr., 47–48
Randolph, Lucille Campbell Green, 49
Ray, James Earl, 24
Robinson, Noah, 5, 6
Roosevelt, Franklin D., 58–59

Truman, Harry S., 59–60

Warren, Earl, 38
Washington, Booker T., 50
White, George, 54, 55
White, Jane, 57
White, Leah Gladys Powell, 57
White, Madeline, 54
White, Walter, 17, 54–60
White, Walter, Jr., 57
White, William, 49

✎ Picture Credits ❦

Collection of the Supreme Court of the United States, p. 33; Culver Pictures, p. 54; Library of Congress, cover; Schomburg Center for Research in Black Culture, New York Public Library, Astor, Lenox, and Tilden Foundations, pp. 12, 47; UPI/Bettmann, pp. 5, 19, 26, 40

RICHARD RENNERT has edited the nearly 100 volumes in Chelsea House's award-winning BLACK AMERICANS OF ACHIEVEMENT series, which tells the stories of black men and women who have helped shape the course of modern history. He is also the author of several sports biographies, including *Henry Aaron*, *Jesse Owens*, and *Jackie Robinson*. He is a graduate of Haverford College in Haverford, Pennsylvania.